The Trenton Commanders

as
Noted in Hessian Diaries

Johann Gottlieb Rall * George Washington

Translated and Compiled by
Bruce E. Burgoyne

HERITAGE BOOKS
2012

HERITAGE BOOKS
AN IMPRINT OF HERITAGE BOOKS, INC.

Books, CDs, and more—Worldwide

For our listing of thousands of titles see our website
at
www.HeritageBooks.com

Published 2012 by
HERITAGE BOOKS, INC.
Publishing Division
100 Railroad Ave. #104
Westminster, Maryland 21157

International Standard Book Numbers
Paperbound: 978-0-7884-0661-4
Clothbound: 978-0-7884-9269-3

The Trenton Commanders

Washington and Rall
As noted in Hessian Diaries

- - - - - - -

Translated and Compiled by
Bruce E. Burgoyne

- - - - - - -

In the closing days of December 1776, the American colonists must have feared that their bold declaration of independence would soon be only an insignificant, minor event, in the history of English rule in the New World.

The remnants of the American army in Pennsylvania, led by General George Washington, were fading away and in a few days would apparently cease to exist. Across the Delaware River, the English forces had gone into winter quarters and were awaiting the start of a final campaign in the spring of the coming year, when they would crush any remaining American force. Chance had placed a brigade of Hessian hirelings in the most exposed English outpost at Trenton. The commander was a Hessian colonel of demonstrated courage and fighting ability, Johann Gottlieb Rall, hero of White Plains and Fort Washington, battles which had driven the Americans out of the New York area.

However, on 26 December the course of history was to take a sharp and sudden change when the two commanders clashed. Washington's army of some 6,000 men crossed the Delaware River in a blinding winter storm and attacked Rall's brigade of about 1,500 men, consisting of three regiments, Lossberg, Knyphausen , and Rall, plus a few jaegers and some English light horse troops. In the fighting which followed the Americans had only a handful of casualties, including James Monroe, later to be the fifth president of the United States. Hessian casualties amounted to about 900 men killed, wounded, and captured, including Colonel Rall, wounded during the battle, who died the same day.

The usual description of Washington, which all American school children are taught, is that he was a tall, dominating figure, who overawed everyone with his presence. Likewise, the description of Colonel Rall, as taught in our schools, is that he was a drunken, overbearing, brute of a man, who considered the American soldiers unfit to be called such. It is true that he had a poor opinion of the Americans as fighting men, but in the following pages the reader will find an indication that neither Washington nor Rall were quite what we were taught in school.

- - - - - - - -

The "Hessian" soldiers kept, and there are still available, numerous diaries in which they recorded their impressions of America and Americans, as well as their daily military activity. My translation of some of these documents has provided opinions and descriptions concerning both of the senior commanders at Trenton, and because he was the victor I shall start with the Hessian comments about Washington.

Private Johann Conrad Doehla, of the Ansbach-Bayreuth contingent of Hessians, never saw Washington, except possibly at the surrender at Yorktown. Nevertheless, on 4 January 1779, he recorded a lengthy description of Washington. "As this American field commander plays an important role in the present war, and already so many incorrect descriptions of this person have been made, therefore I will share the following from a believable American description of the person and character of Washington.

General Washington

"This great General Washington is of medium but respectable height, has a martial face, and although already old, namely more than fifty, he is still in good, blooming health. His entire bearing is very reserved and careful, not profuse in words, and more loving of loneliness than great sociability, in order to use the time for thought and speculation. Therefore, he often rides out entirely alone on a favorite white horse. Outside the camp he has no more than a single servant, and when he returns to camp he is accompanied up to his tent by only a few riders of his Light Horse, or Light Cavalry. At New York he often visits his field and camp posts all by himself, and often converses with a sentry for a full quarter of an hour. When he has something great and important on his mind, he allows, even then, only a few, but [they are] the best and most intelligent officers whom he trusts to come to him, and [he] sends his suggested plan at the same time around to a few others in order to solicit, in this manner, the advice of each individual without having imposed his judgment. He is not the least bit proud or arrogant; often speaks kindly and in a friendly manner with a sentry just as with a staff officer. Toward strangers he is reserved, even if they are recommended to him by Congress. He sharply punishes all negligence in duty, but toward recruits he is kind and forgiving until they have mastered the exercises and Articles of War. Toward spies he has a great abhorrence, although he himself must often employ the same. The Indians and savages, because of their cruel barbarities, are disgusting to him. He is soft-hearted and seldom attends military punishments, and then with displeasure, and he either pardons the criminal or takes another way to avoid such unpleasant sights. The art of war is his primary study. His suggestions are well thought out. He is especially careful in all situations to insure a retreat. His chief characteristics are decisiveness, stability, patience, and secretiveness. He rewards good conduct on the spot. Toward the prisoners who fall into his hands, he is very humane and attentive to their good treatment. In eating and drinking, supposedly he is very moderate, and his relaxation and pleasure consists of having a few glasses of punch. Also, he is married and has a beautiful wife, who accompanies him at all times with the army in the field. He also has a son, seventeen years old, who is already a lieutenant colonel in the French service."[1]

The same description, nearly word for word with any change the result of translating from English to German and then back to English, appeared one year later, on 4 March 1780, in the *New Hampshire Gazette*. Obviously the item circulated for some time throughout the American colonies.[2]

Two of the Hessian officers captured at Trenton actually had an opportunity to see and speak, one at some length, with Washington. Both were lieutenants of the Hesse-Cassel contingent. I know nothing more about Lieutenant Jakob Piel than what is recorded in his diary; Lieutenant Andreas Wiederhold remained in military service after the Revolutionary War, eventually becoming a general officer in the Portuguese service. Both men were excellent map makers and copies of their maps are still in existence.[3] Following their capture, Piel noted a get together with William Alexander, Lord Stirling, who escorted the officers to meet General Washington.

On 28 December 1776, Piel wrote in his diary, "That one, [Washington], received us very politely, but we understood very little of what he said because he spoke nothing but English - a language which at that time none of us handled well.[4] In the face of this man nothing of the great man showed for which he would be noted. His eyes have no fire, but a slight smile in his expression when he spoke inspired love and respect. He kept four of our officers for the noon meal and the rest of us ate with Lord Stirling."

Apparently Wiederhold was one of the four officers who ate that day with General Washington, as the lieutenant recorded the following comments about Washington in his diary on 28 December 1776.[5] As stated therein, "General Washington is a polite and refined man, seldom speaks, and has a cunning physiognomy. He is not especially tall, but also not short, but rather of middle height with a good body. His face bears a resemblance to that of Captain [Georg Wilhelm] von Biesenrodt of the Knyphausen Regiment."

Obviously Piel and Wiederhold were not overly-impressed with the American general, although they may have written down their descriptions, not wanting to record too much praise about the man who had just defeated them so decisively in battle. Otherwise, both descriptions are similar in content.

The same can not be said about their post-capture opinion of Colonel Rall. It is to be noted in the following comments that Wiederhold could find nothing good about Colonel Rall and placed the entire blame for the defeat on the dead colonel. Piel, on the other hand, recorded very sympathetic and favorable comments about Rall's character, while acknowledging that Rall was simply out of his depth as a brigade commander, and that General Howe should have expected nothing more than Rall's inability to hold the important position at Trenton.

Before presenting the opinions of the officers however, there are a few incidents, recorded by Johannes Reuber, a private in Rall's own regiment, which indicate the favorable, even affectionate, view of Rall held by the enlisted men of the regiment.[6]

On 21 August 1776, [Reuber's dates are often wrong], having been assigned to the forces on Long Island, the Rall Regiment " 'had the duty of protecting the flag'. We now stood in the line before Flatbush and the entire army moved forward toward a woods in which we could see a rebel corps of fifty men with flags flying, coming toward the Rall Regiment. Colonel Rall ordered the regiment to fire at the Americans. When they saw what was in store, they surrendered and dropped their weapons, calling out, 'Pardon', and lay all their equipment down before the Rall Regiment.

"A non-commissioned officer of our regiment seized the rebel flag and wanted to present it to Colonel Rall at the head of the regiment. Before this could be accomplished, Brigadier General [Werner] von Mirbach came riding from the left flank and tried to take the American flag, captured by our regiment, from the hands of the non-commissioned officer, and claim the prize for himself as brigade general.

"However, the colonel said, 'Nothing doing, general. My grenadiers captured the flag and they shall keep it, and no one will take it from them.'

"Therefore they separated in anger and both intended to enter a complaint at headquarters, But what happened? Colonel Rall was named inspector general of the brigade."

On 26 September 1776, at White Plains, "The Old Lossberg Regiment had to advance toward a stream, the Bronx Creek, which lay in a valley. However, it suffered great losses of wounded and had to pull back. The Rall Grenadier Regiment had the left wing from which Colonel Rall saw the situation, which now existed. Therefore, as the Americans were before us, Colonel Rall ordered his regiment to turn, to immediately descend the hill through the water, through the Bronx Creek, and again up the hill where the Old Lossberg Regiment stood, and united with the other English and Hessians.

"We could see above us on the hill that the Americans were advancing, and also meant to occupy this hill. However, they were unable to force our retreat. We were able to move behind the Americans and our army obtained the advantage."

The regiment was heavily engaged again on 16 November 1776, during the attack on Fort Washington, although Reuber recorded the action as taking place on 17 November. "At daybreak the Americans became aware of us but it was too late. Suddenly the two warships on either side opened fire against Fort Washington. At the same time the land attack began with cannon fire and ship fire, all the regiments and corps marched forward in order to clamber up the hills and stone cliffs. One fell down, still alive, the next one was shot dead. We had to pull ourselves up by grasping the wild boxtree bushes and could not stand upright until we finally arrived on top of the height. As the trees and large rocks were encountered close upon one another and [the terrain] did not become more even, Colonel Rall commanded, 'All who are my grenadiers, forward march!' All the drums beat a march. The musicians played a march. Suddenly everyone still alive shouted, 'Hurrah!' Then everyone was at once mixed together, Americans and Hessians were as one. No more shots were fired, but everyone ran toward the defenses. As we approached the height where the Americans had a trench around the defenses, we had to halt. Then the Americans pressed on at a run to the defenses, but we stopped them. 'You are prisoners of war.' General von Knyphausen called on the fort to surrender and two hours later the rebels surrendered Fort Washington, and all munitions and provisions in and outside the fort were turned over to General von Knyphausen. Everyone had to lay down his weapons and after this transpired, the Rall and Old Lossberg Regiments formed two lines, between which [the rebels] had to march."

The regiment then followed the retreating American army as far as the Delaware River, but went into winter quarters at Trenton when that river could not be crossed due to a lack of boats. The Reuber account of the movement and activities of the Rall Regiment continues [with wrong dates, as usual], without finding fault with Colonel Rall's decisions or conduct. On 22 December, Reuber wrote, "During the night the black Negroes and yellow dogs planned to attack us at reveille, but nothing came of it. A detachment at the Delaware was attacked by Americans who crossed the Delaware to our side, set some houses on fire, and then retreated back across the Delaware to their side. Again everything was quiet, but at night the companies had to enter the alert houses as usual and stack their weapons before the night posts."

On 23 December his diary continued. "A 100-man detachment from our three regiments was ordered to a bridge across the Delaware not far from Philadelphia and this prompted the inhabitants to intensify their alarm of a rebel attack. However, who could have imagined that it could have come to such a point."

Then on 24 December, "on the afternoon of the Christmas Saturday, three English regiments came to Trenton from Princeton in order to reinforce us. When they paraded before Colonel Rall's quarters in the city and reported to him, they were required to turn about and march back to Princeton. During the evening a 100-man picket was stationed around the city. In the dark of the night there were suddenly alarm shots at our outposts. An American patrol, or advance guard, had approached too close to our outposts. As they then fired upon our outposts, all three regiments had to move out. Colonel Rall took two companies and one cannon and marched through the woods in order to reconnoiter around the outposts, but nothing happened and he returned. After his return with the two companies, everyone had to enter the alert houses and occupy our positions."

However, on 25 December, [Reuber's date should be 26 December], "on the first [second] blessed Christmas morning, at daybreak, the Americans marched against our 100-man picket and at the same time, the Americans fired on our outposts. At the first salvo, we turned out from our alert houses and went to the alert areas to form and prepare our battle formations. Now the rebels pressed in on us. At Colonel Rall's quarters there was a wall of boards before which our two cannons stood in the street, opposite the seven American cannons, and they destroyed one of the American gun carriages. Now the Americans charged Colonel Rall's quarters, overran it, and took the cannons from the regiment. Then the colonel charged with his grenadiers. Although we went against enemy cannons, we retook our cannons, and retired from the city into the fields. Now Colonel Rall commanded, 'All those who are my grenadiers, charge!' and they stormed against the city as the Americans retreated before us. However, after we had entered the city, the rebels, in three lines, marched around us and as we again tried to retreat, they again brought seven cannons into the main street. We had to go past them, but things went badly for us before we could accomplish this purpose. If the colonel had not been so seriously wounded, they would not have taken us alive, even though they were 15,000 men and our brigade was only 1,700 men strong. We were too weak, the headquarters had been lost, and in the end all was lost. With his last breath he thought about his grenadiers and asked General Washington to take nothing from them except that which was considered as weapons, but it was taken and kept. It had now reached the point where as quickly as possible they rounded us up."

Lieutenant Piel, adjutant of the von Lossberg Regiment, provides the following account of the battle and Colonel Rall's conduct on that day. "**26 December** - The Rall Brigade, since the fourteenth of the month, had occupied the small city of Trenton on the Delaware. The enemy stood on the opposite side of the river, and because they had boats and we had none, they could cross at any point and harass us. Yesterday evening, at twilight, they attacked our outposts, but pulled back almost at once, after wounding six of our men.

"Between seven and eight o'clock this morning we were formally attacked by a corps of 6,000 to 7,000 men under General [George] Washington. Our outposts soon found it necessary to retreat and we barely had time to take up our weapons before we lost many people in the city, due to the small arms and cannon fire of the enemy. We were surrounded on all sides but defended ourselves for two full hours, until the Knyphausen Regiment was cut off from us; our weapons, because of the rain and snow could no longer be fired; and the rebels fired on us from all the houses. There remained no other choice for us but to surrender. The Lossberg Regiment lost about seventy men, dead and wounded, in this engagement. Among the first were Captains [Johann Kaspar] Riess and [Friedrich Wilhelm] von Benning and Lieutenant [Georg Christian] Kimm. Captain [Ernst Eberhard] von Alten-Bockum and Lieutenants [Ernst Christian] Schwabe and [Hermann Henrich Georg] Zoll were wounded. We had only Colonel Rall to thank for our complete misfortune. It never struck him that the rebels might attack us, and therefore he had made no preparations against an attack. I must concede that on the whole we had a very poor opinion of the rebels, who previously had never successfully opposed us. Our brigadier was too proud to retreat one step from such an enemy, as from the start, there was no other choice for us but to retreat.

"Colonel Rall was mortally wounded and died the same evening, satisfied that it was not necessary for him to outlive his honor.

"General [William] Howe judged the man from an incorrect historical view. Otherwise, he would hardly have entrusted to him such an important post as Trenton.

"Colonel Rall was truly born to be a soldier, but not a general. This man, who by capturing Fort Washington, earned the greatest honor because he was under the leadership of a great general, lost his entire reputation at Trenton where he was himself the general. He had courage enough to undertake the most audacious task. However, he lacked the presence of mind which it is necessary to have in an engagement such as the attack on Trenton. His love of live was too great. A thought came to him, then another, so that he could not settle on a firm decision. Considered as a private individual, he merited the highest respect. He was generous, magnanimous, hospitable, and polite to everyone; never grovelling before his superiors, but indulgent to his subordinates. To his servants he was more friend than master. He was an exceptional friend of music and a pleasant companion."

Lieutenant Wiederhold had no such kind words for Colonel Rall. His diary entries for the period covering the attack on Trenton reflect a bitterness, for which Colonel Rall is held solely responsible, despite Wiederhold's almost single-handed efforts to avert the tragedy. Commencing on 14 December the Wiederhold diary gives the description of the surprise attack and Rall's failure as a commander in the words which have left Colonel Rall as a failure as a military leader and a nearly inhumane individual.

"**14 December** - We marched to the famous place Trenton, which I shall never forget in my life, and where our all too easy-going brigadier took us because of his conduct, as it is said. How much better off he would have been if he had not sought, and would not have received the undeserved praise that had been directed to him. He might have kept his reputation. However, in truth everyone lay in pleasant quarters. Our army's exhausted and destitute of small clothes soldiers could recover even less here than in the field. The duties were exceptional, guard duty, special detachments, picket duty without end, even though they were unnecessary and served no purpose, but only senseless employment throughout the day in the vicinity of the brigadier's quarters. Whether the guards and detachments were relieved, whether the soldiers were wearing pants, shoes, shirt, etc., or nothing, whether or not ammunition was wasted; these things were immaterial, and he never inquired about them.

"But the hautboists! They were his thing, and as the main watch was six or eight houses from his quarters, they could not play long enough. The officer had first to march, with music, around the neighborhood church, which stood near his quarters and into which a small doorway led.

"This looked like a Catholic procession. Nothing was missing except the flag with a cross and a number of small boys and girls, singing at the head. He always followed the parade as far as the guard post, so as to hear the music during the change over. Another commander, like him, during this time, would have met with the staff officers and others coming from duty, to discuss the well-being and security of the garrison and other matters.

"Toward two o'clock the detachments were relieved and about four o'clock the pickets. All officers and non-commissioned officers had to be present then at his quarters so that it looked like an important headquarters. The cannons, which should have been on the street or at places where they were ready for instant use, had to be brought to stand before the quarters, and every morning two of them had to be taken to the upper part of town so that there was a constant uproar and commotion.

"Personally, he enjoyed himself until late at night, then peacefully went to bed, slept until nine o'clock, then paraded between ten and eleven o'clock, and then entered his quarters. He sat reclining in his usual bath and therefore the watch often had to wait half an hour to be formed.

"Not the least precaution was taken, no assembly point nor alert system was prepared in case of attack. Even less thought was given that an attack was even possible. Major von Dechow made the excellent suggestion that some defensive positions be thrown up and the cannons placed therein so that everything would be ready in case of an attack, and the best defense could be made.

"'Unnecessary nonsense', [in a much more vulgar expression], was the colonel's reply. 'Let them come! Why defenses? We will go at them with the bayonet!'

"Major Dechow sought to persist and said, 'Colonel, it does not cost anything. If it does not help, it also does no harm.', and suggested I undertake this task, and asked where and how he wished it done. He repeated his first words, laughed at both of us, and walked away.

"He believed the name Rall was so frightening and stronger than the works of Vauban and Coehorn, against which no rebel would attack. A clever man to command a corps and more so, a courageous man to defend a position which stood so close to the enemy, where he had more than 100 advantages. He did everything without consideration and forethought. Proof of this is that once he wished to send a letter, possibly of no great significance, with two dragoons to General [Alexander] Leslie at Princeton. They were fired upon in a woods by a running party of possibly only farmers, which resulted in one dead. The other returned and reported this. **Note:** This occurred about three miles from Trenton on the road to Maidenhead.

"He immediately ordered a captain, three officers, and 100 men with a cannon and the necessary artillerymen, including me, to deliver this letter. The weather was exceptionally bad. We delivered our letter, slept on God's earth during the night, and returned home early the next morning without seeing or hearing anything. The Englanders made great fun of us, and it was truly laughable, because a non-commissioned officer and fifteen men were adequate to execute this because it was to our rear, and the whole distance between both garrisons was only about eleven miles.

"When we marched from Kingston to Maidenhead, Major von Dechow reported to him that as many troops had fallen behind, he would like to make a brief halt so that they could rejoin us. He [the colonel] answered that they would catch up; he had to and would proceed, even if he was only able to take half of the troops with him. So it was, and during the following days some from his regiment caught up.

"Where the enemy always caused us false alarms, he sent more than enough troops, and where the actual attacks were to be expected and actually did occur, he gave little consideration. A non-commissioned officer with twenty men stood in the road where the attack took place, and as this post, on the previous evening, had been attacked by an enemy patrol, on orders of General Washington, under the command of a captain who was to have made only a reconnaissance, but with the specific order not to engage, but in case he was discovered to pull back as quietly as possible. However, this captain believed he would demonstrate his bravery if he made an attack and wounded four or five men of the non-commissioned officer's post. The entire garrison was alerted, placed under arms, and a division of the Rall Regiment was sent to see what was happening. That was all that he did except for sending me and another nine men and a non-commissioned officer to reinforce that post.

"The division had already returned before I arrived at my post, and had not gone very far. A more vigilant commander would have issued orders to reconnoiter all the roads as far as the river and the ferries to determine that everything was quiet and peaceful, or to attack the enemy, and not return until this was done. This would have revealed the whole plan and turned the scale.

"As soon as I arrived at my post, I set out seven posts, as well as I could during the night and sent out one patrol after the other to prevent being surprised, as shown in the accompanying plan [not available]. The night passed quietly. About an hour after sunrise, after my morning patrols had been back for some time and had reported everything quiet, and the jaegers under my command had pulled back from their night posts, I was attacked out of the woods, along the road from Johns Ferry. If I had not stepped out of the picket hut and seen the enemy, they would possibly have been upon me before I could take up arms, because my guards were not alert enough because it was a holiday.[7]

"Furthermore, the advance guard did not expect the enemy, but a patrol from Captain [Johann Henrich] Bruebach's picket, which had not yet returned. I had taken up arms in time and awaited the enemy, but I too assumed it to be a raiding party. They fired three salvos at me and the seventeen men that I had under arms. After the third round I gave the order to fire and engaged them until I was nearly surrounded by several battalions. I then pulled back, under a steady fire, to the Alten-Bockum Company, which had assembled during our engagement and had formed at an angle across the street before the captain's quarters.

"I placed myself on the right wing and continued to fire individually. However, at the mentioned place, it was necessary, in order not to be cut off from the garrison, to retreat toward the garrison as no one came to see what was happening, nor to reinforce and assist us, even though the Rall Regiment was the duty watch on this night. I positioned myself in the city at the first houses and fired at the enemy, who were forming for battle on the city's heights.

"At this time the brigadier made his appearance and did not know which way to turn. I considered it to be my responsibility, as he did not know what had happened outside the city, to report what I had seen and knew, and said the enemy was strong, that they were not only above the city, but were already around it on both the left and right sides, so that he should not consider this to be only a minor thing. He asked how strong the enemy was. I replied that I could not say with certainty as I had to give my attention to my men, but that I had seen four or five battalions moving out of the woods and had received fire from three of them before I had to retire from my post.

"He called to his regiment then, before mounting his horse. 'Forward march! Advance! Advance!' and staggered back and forth without knowing what he was doing, thereby losing the time and the still available moment to move to another location, honorably and without injury. He moved out with his regiment to the right of the city, under the apple trees, first wanting to attack along the Princeton Road. When the loss of the baggage, which had been left in the city, was mentioned to him (I do not know by whom), he changed his mind and attacked toward the voluntarily surrendered city with his and the Lossberg Regiment. What nonsense this was! To try to retake, with 600 to 700 men, a city which was of no value and which had been left ten or fifteen minutes previously, which was now filled with 3,000 to 4,000 enemy, in houses, and behind the walls and fences. An only slightly more clever and less talented but knowledgeable person could see the weakness here.

"He can not be forgiven for the following four mistakes. 1) That he did not know the enemy was in the vicinity with such a strength and able to attack his garrison across a wide river covered with ice, with so much difficulty that it took sixteen hours, after having been warned and having gotten wind of it. 2) That after the pickets had been attacked the night before and had indications enough, not to have sent strong patrols instantly to reconnoiter the ferries and woods, to seek out the enemy, and to pack and send off all baggage during this time, so as not to be burdened by excessive baggage and equipment. 3) To have had the garrison under arms during the night and to march across the bridge to the heights of the upper city in a position to await the enemy and his undertaking. 4) That after all this neglect and at the time of the surprise, not to have crossed the bridge, and in case this was prevented, to use every effort and means, first to form a solid corps and force a path to a place, which was still possible, from which the garrison could still be saved.

"It is a fact, and if we have learned anything from the experience, that when a person is surprised and initially tries as much as possible to keep the private soldiers from panicking, and then when that happens, and they have partially recovered and seen that the danger is not as great as it appeared initially, it is then possible for an individual to once again set himself straight. But he had neither the disposition nor the necessary resolution, and there was more stupidity than courage in his conduct. If there is not much courage in a commanding officer, but only stupidity, he most often reacts in confusion, with few indications of bravery and [considerable] weakness. This is the true reason that the three battalions were captured. He was twice fatally wounded because of making the ill-considered attack, died the same evening, and lies buried at the Presbyterian Church in this place which he made so famous.

"Sleep well, dear commander! The Americans reportedly erected a marker on his grave later, and wrote the following words, 'Here lies Colonel Rall. His life is over.'

"During the battle a certain character came forth. I do not know what brought it on. I believe a heavy heart. Therefore he went home and lay down in bed. That was sensible. In this mentioned attack, the Lossberg and Rall Regiments became so confused and mixed together that it was impossible to reestablish order. Thereafter, as they were nearly surrounded, they had to surrender.

"Our regiment did not participate with them during the attack, as I heard later when I returned to the regiment with my picket, but had been ordered to cover the flank. After the above two regiments had been repulsed and captured, our regiment sought to secure the bridge, but this was already strongly occupied on both sides, so that it was impossible to move over it. We sought to wade through the water but it was not practical at this point and as two enemy battalions, with four cannons, marched up close in front of us and seized the right flank, which was our only escape, the only possible place of rescue. We had to follow the other two regiments and surrender as prisoners of war.....

"General Lord Stirling assured us that he had no more than 6,000 men and fourteen cannons and two howitzers with him. This was enough to surround 1,000 men as they were not in the best disposition and were under the orders of a careless commander. Our fame and honor, earned at White Plains and Fort Knyphausen suffered a severe blow here.....

"Still, I must say I have no reason to reproach myself. With the seventeen men I had with me, I did all that was possible and all that an honorable man could be responsible for doing. Even the enemy, and especially General Lord Stirling, who commanded the advance guard, and as a result was engaged with me, added his praise and acknowledgment, which is of special worth [as can be attested] by Lieutenant Piel and Lieutenant [Christian] Sobbe, who also dined with him at a midday meal. When I dined with General Washington he made the pleasant compliment , and expressly asked to meet me in order, as he said, to get to know such an excellent officer in person. He had asked about my name and character and noted such on his blackboard, and authorized and offered free access to himself at all times, wherever he might be.....

"But woe to him who is responsible for the misfortune of many honorable men. The loss of all fortune, the unnecessary and meaningless loss of the blood that was spilled, is on his hands and charged to him. Enough about all of that. I wish to Heaven it had not been necessary for me to enter such sad news in my journal. My own loss, although I saved some things, was nevertheless considerable. The honor, gained and previously enjoyed, had made an honorable man grievous and painfully ill.

- - - - - - -

Regardless of how the Hessians reported the battle, or their opinions of the commanders, the outcome of the battle and the facts are quite clear. Washington had struck a master stroke, saved the rebellion, and earned his place in American history. Rall, regardless of whether held in esteem by his men for military courage and humanity, had demonstrated an incompetence as a senior commander which may have been the most significant contribution to England's loss of the American colonies. It is our good fortune that after more than two hundred years, we still have the Hessian reports to help us understand the events and the men who played such important roles in our nation's birth.

- - - - - - -

Notes

1. (p. 3) From *A Hessian Diary of the American Revolution*, by Johann Conrad Doehla. Translated, edited, and with an Introduction by Bruce E. Burgoyne. Copyright 1990 by the University of Oklahoma Press, pp. 99-100.

2. (p. 3) *The Diary of the Revolution; A centennial Volume embracing the Current Events in Our Country's History from 1775 to 1781, As described by American, British, and Tory Contemporaries,* Compiled by Frank Moore, The J.B. Burr Publishing Company (Hartford, 1876), pp 775-776. Citing the New Hampshire Gazette, 4 March 1780.

3. (p. 4) Maps by Piel and Wiederhold, depicting the Battle of Trenton, are to be found in William S. Stryker's *The Battles of Trenton and Princeton, (Cambridge, 1898)*.

4. (p. 4) Quotes from the Piel diary are based on translation of a German manuscript in the Bancroft Collection of the New York Public Library by Bruce E. Burgoyne.

5. (p. 4) Quotes from the Wiederhold diary are based on translation of a German manuscript in the Bancroft Collection of the New York Public Library by Bruce E. Burgoyne.

6. (p. 5) Quotes from the Reuber diary are based on translation of a German manuscript in the Bancroft Collection of the New York Public Library by Bruce E. Burgoyne.

7. (p. 12) The Europeans consider both 25 and 26 December as Christmas holidays.

Other Heritage Books by Bruce E. Burgoyne:

*Aboard a Dutch Troop Transport: A Diary Written by
Captain Ludwig Alberti of the Waldeck 5th Battalion*

*A Hessian Officer's Diary of the American Revolution
Translated from an Anonymous Ansbach-Bayreuth Diary and the Prechtel Diary*

*Canada During the American Revolutionary War: Lieutenant Friedrich Julius von Papet's
Journal of the Sea Voyage to North America and the Campaign Conducted There*

CD: A Hessian Diary of the American Revolution

CD: A Hessian Officer's Diary of The American Revolution

*CD: A Hessian Report on the People, the Land, the War of Eighteenth Century
America, as Noted in the Diary of Chaplain Philipp Waldeck, 1776-1780*

CD: Ansbach-Bayreuth Diaries from the Revolutionary War

CD: Canada During the America Revolutionary War

CD: Diaries of Two Ansbach Jaegers

CD: The Hessian Collection, Volume 1: Revolutionary War Era

CD: They Also Served. Women with the Hessian Auxiliaries

CD: Waldeck Soldiers of the American Revolutionary War

Defeat, Disaster, and Dedication

Diaries of Two Ansbach Jaegers

*Eighteenth Century America (A Hessian Report on the People, the Land, the War)
as Noted in the Diary of Chaplain Philipp Waldeck (1776-1780)*

Enemy Views: The American Revolutionary War as Recorded by the Hessian Participants

*English Army and Navy Lists Compiled During the American Revolutionary War by
Ansbach-Bayreuth Lieutenant Johann Ernst Prechtel*

*Georg Pausch's Journal and Reports of the Campaign in America, as
Translated from the German Manuscript in the Lidgerwood Collection in the
Morristown Historical Park Archives, Morristown, New Jersey*

*Hesse-Hanau Order Books, a Diary and Roster: A Collection of Items
Concerning the Hesse-Hanau Contingent of "Hessians" Fighting
Against the American Colonists in the Revolutionary War*

Hessian Chaplains: Their Diaries and Duties

Hessian Letters and Journals and a Memoir

Journal of a Hessian Grenadier Battalion

Journal of the Hesse-Cassel Jaeger Corps

Journal of the Prince Charles Regiment
Translated by Bruce E. Burgoyne; Edited by Dr. Marie E. Burgoyne

*Most Illustrious Hereditary Prince: Letters to Their Prince
from Members of Hesse-Hanau Military Contingent in the
Service of England During the American Revolution*

www.ingramcontent.com/pod-product-compliance
Lightning Source LLC
Chambersburg PA
CBHW060609030426
42337CB00019B/3678